To: ~~Jim~~ Berryman

From: E_____ ___ MIT

With our _____ ___ and
appreciation for ~~the~~
great series of lectures
on Tomography;

uh. ~~Say~~ Bishop

Rick ~~Gibson~~

Delaine Thompson

___ ___

Jeffrey A. Meredith

Lisa Block

Ted Charette

Bob Cicerone

Wenjie Dong

Arthur Cheng

___

E Shtatland

Anton Dainty

Bill Rodi

Richard Coates.

Karl Ellefsen

Batakrishna Mandal.

Sergio Kostek

Xiaomin Zhao

Massachusetts Institute of Technology
Cambridge, Massachusetts

Edited by James B. Patrick.

Designed by Donald G. Paulhus.

Printed in Japan.

Published by Fort Church Publishers, Inc.
Little Compton, Rhode Island 02837

MIT
A PORTRAIT

Photography by Robert Llewellyn
Introduction by John I. Mattill

". . . a university polarized around science, technology, and the arts."

Robert Llewellyn's photographs in this book make clear his fascination with what may seem to be two different institutions brought together under the ponderous and much too narrow title, Massachusetts Institute of Technology. M.I.T.'s Killian Court is a classic academic façade, to which Llewellyn returned in every season as if to establish that he was, in fact, in a university environment. But behind this formal yet congenial façade Llewellyn found teaching and research in high technology and its social context that seemed part of another world – an incongruity, almost a nonsequitur.

What needs to be said, with more emphasis than the photographs can convey, is that these are two contrasting images of a single institution – an educational enterprise significantly different in both concept and realization from any other in the world. It is different precisely because it alloys into one the academic tradition represented by its façade with the technological revolution that is glimpsed through open doors everywhere inside these great buildings.

The uniqueness of the Massachusetts Institute of Technology can be traced directly to the break from tradition that M.I.T.'s founder proclaimed as he sought support for his fledgling enterprise in the middle of the nineteenth century. In contrast to the universities of the time, founder William Barton Rogers conceived in M.I.T. an institution devoted to "practical science," listing specifically such fields as machinery, manufactures, chemical analysis, mineral exploration and mining, and locomotion. But he insisted that his school should "embrace full courses of instruction in all the principles of physical truth" – mechanics, electricity and magnetism, thermodynamics, and chemistry – as a basic foundation for its students' understanding of technology. "The true and only practicable object of a polytechnic school is, as I conceive," wrote Rogers, "the teaching, not of the minute details and manipulations of the arts . . . but the inculcation of those scientific principles which form the basis and explanation of them. . . . There is no branch of practical industry, whether in the arts of construction, manufactures, or agriculture, which is not capable of being better practiced, and even of being improved in its process, through the knowledge of its connections with physical truths and laws."

With remarkable clairvoyance, Rogers promised that his M.I.T. would become "a great institution comprehending the whole field of physical science and the arts with the auxiliary branches of mathematics and modern languages, (that) would soon overtop the universities of the land in the accuracy and extent of its teaching in all branches of positive knowledge."

The institution of Llewellyn's photographs is remarkably close to that vision its founder proclaimed some 150 years ago. The famous phrase attributed to President Emeritus James R. Killian, Jr., '26, puts it succinctly and in a way that has caught the attention of many: ". . . a university polarized around science, technology, and the arts."

Implicit if not explicit in Rogers' advocacy of M.I.T. was the increasing role that technology promised to have in the American economy and, indeed, in daily life, and the effect that an institution such as M.I.T. might have on these changes. Indeed, Rogers could hardly have foreseen the rapidly growing opportunities that came to M.I.T. beginning late in the nineteenth century. Here were organized the first curricula in at least five technical fields that we now take for granted – electrical engineering, sanitary engineering, naval architecture and marine engineering, aeronautical engineering, and meteorology. Long before their significance was appreciated outside the Institute, there were laboratories in operations research, servomechanisms, cryogenics, food technology, cognitive science, nuclear physics and nuclear engineering, artificial intelligence, and many more. From M.I.T. came a parade of such American leaders as Godfrey L. Cabot, '81, Bradley Dewey, '09, James H. Doolittle, '24, Donald W. Douglas, '14, Pierre S. du Pont, '90, Eric Hodgins, '22, Jerome C. Hunsaker, '12, Frank B. Jewett, '03, Arthur D. Little, '85, Charles T. Main, '76, Willard F. Rockwell, '08, Alfred P. Sloan, Jr., '95 and Gerard Swope, '95 – to name but a few.

How it was that M.I.T. so flowered during its first half-century is a question to which there is no single answer: its faculty were chosen well, its students bright and motivated, its location – Boston – a center of cultural and technical development. Beyond these, however, comes a more provocative suggestion from Professor Emeritus Elting E. Morison, the first holder of the Elizabeth and James Killian 1926 Professorship before his retirement in 1975. In a private communication to Dr. Killian, Professor Morison comments on the importance of what he believes is the special attitude toward learning that has prevailed at M.I.T. since its advocacy by Dr. Rogers:

"Historically, the object of most scholarship in traditional universities has been to obtain a more accurate description and fuller understanding of . . . the nature of things and of human experience," writes Morison. "But at M.I.T. the aim, for much of its history, has been to learn what was needed to improve the machinery of society – to make things work better. As a result the Institute tended to become more directly engaged in the world around than did its older counterparts. Because of both their work and their caste of thought, it was natural for those in the Institute to take large parts in what was happening."

Today, when so much of the essential structure of life is determined by technological development, M.I.T.'s role is a very special one. The Institute makes major contributions to science and to the technology that flows from it, and to strategies for their management. No institution has a larger, better qualified faculty devoted to this work, and to teaching students who are themselves outstandingly qualified. But the Institute's purpose is still to "take a large part in what is happening," to be a leader in scientific and technological change and in understanding and capitalizing on its consequences. As President Paul E. Gray, '54, said in his Inaugural Address in 1980, "We need to understand – and to engage – the larger social, cultural, and historical domains of which science and technology are a part. We must be a sanctuary for the constructive criticism of the technological enterprise and of the larger society. These principles must be built into the academic programs of our students, and they must be reflected in the lives and activities of all who choose to be a part of this institution . . ."

John I. Mattill
Editor, *Technology Review*

Spring sunshine on the Maclaurin Building steps

The President's House, 111 Memorial Drive   Killian Court detail   11

Main entrance, 77 Massachusetts Avenue

The Maclaurin Building (Building 10) Lobby

Sails on the Charles

Institute Professor Harold E. Edgerton, '27 in Strobe Alley

Memorial Drive has become dormitory row

Building 2 from Killian Court

Domes: Rogers, Maclaurin, and Green Buildings

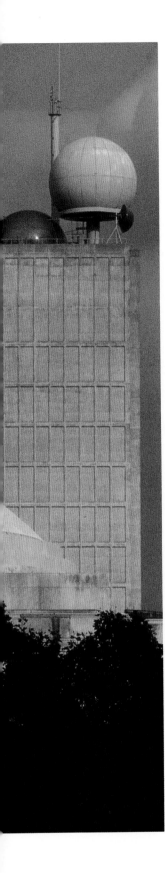

Three-dimensional hologram in the Media Laboratory   23

Whitaker College and the Wiesner Building

The Green and Landau Buildings

Sunset on the Charles River

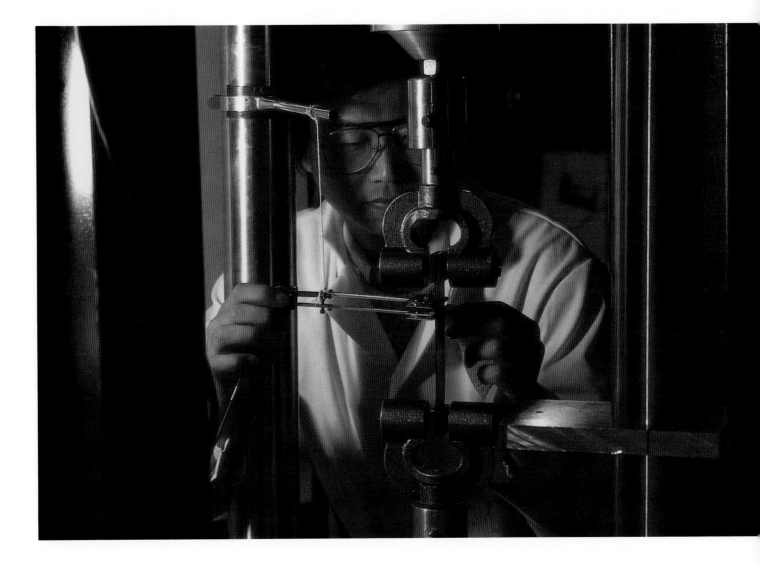

Materials: crack propagation in rubber composite   *Overleaf:* Pops Concert on the Boston Esplanade

Looking west from the Whitaker College Buildings

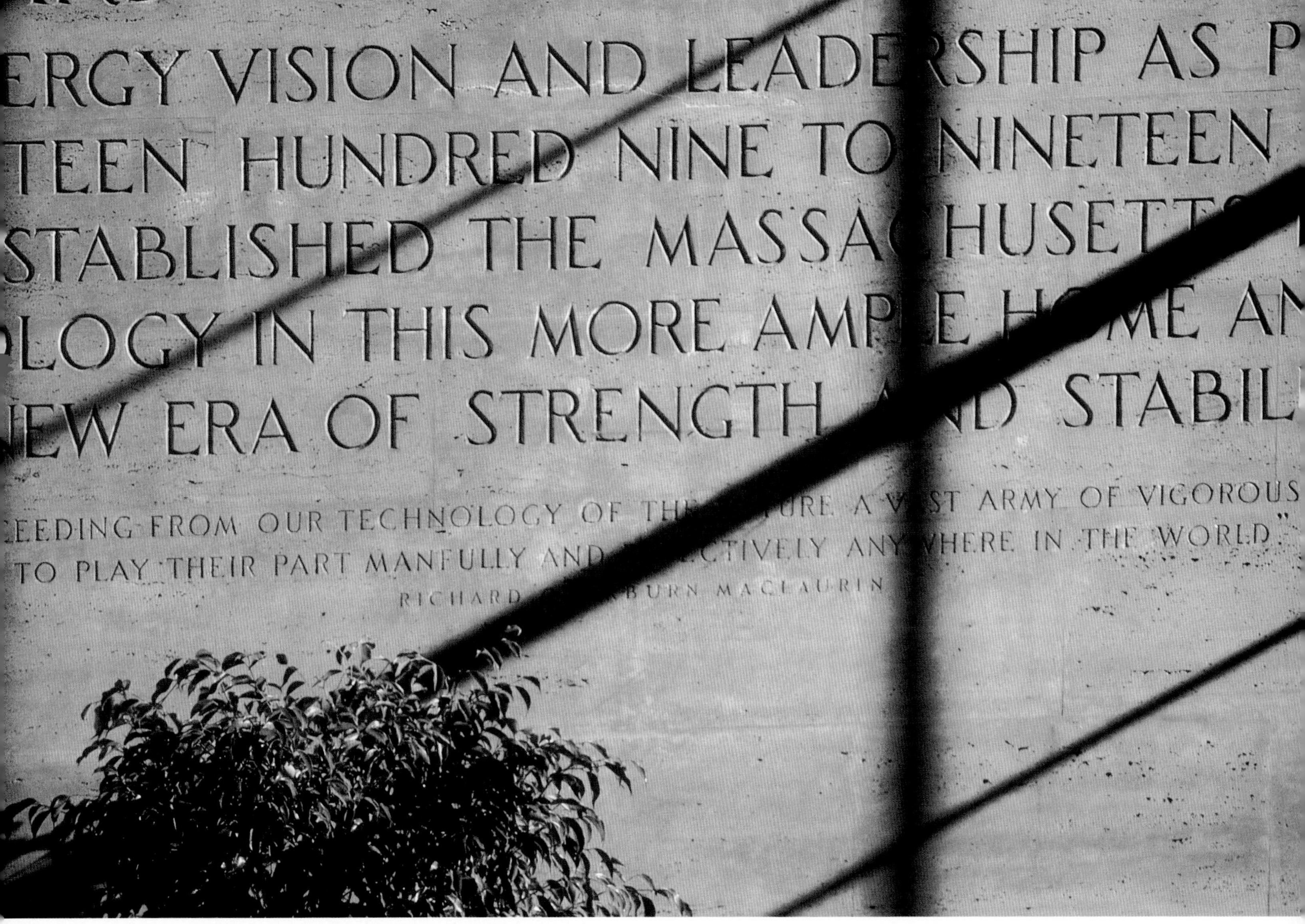

ARD. COCKBURN

ERGY VISION AND LEADERSHIP AS P

TEEN HUNDRED NINE TO NINETEEN

STABLISHED THE MASSACHUSETTS

OLOGY IN THIS MORE AMPLE HOME AN

EW ERA OF STRENGTH AND STABIL

EEDING FROM OUR TECHNOLOGY OF THE   URE A V ST ARMY OF VIGOROUS
TO PLAY THEIR PART MANFULLY AND   CTIVELY ANYWHERE IN THE WORLD"
RICHARD   BURN MACLAURIN

The Charles River Basin

Francis Bitter National Magnet Laboratory

Winter sun in the Maclaurin Lobby   *Overleaf:* The Haystack Radio Telescope, Westford, Mass.

Architectural design studio

Toroidal confinement research in the Plasma Fusion Center

At the Pierce Boathouse

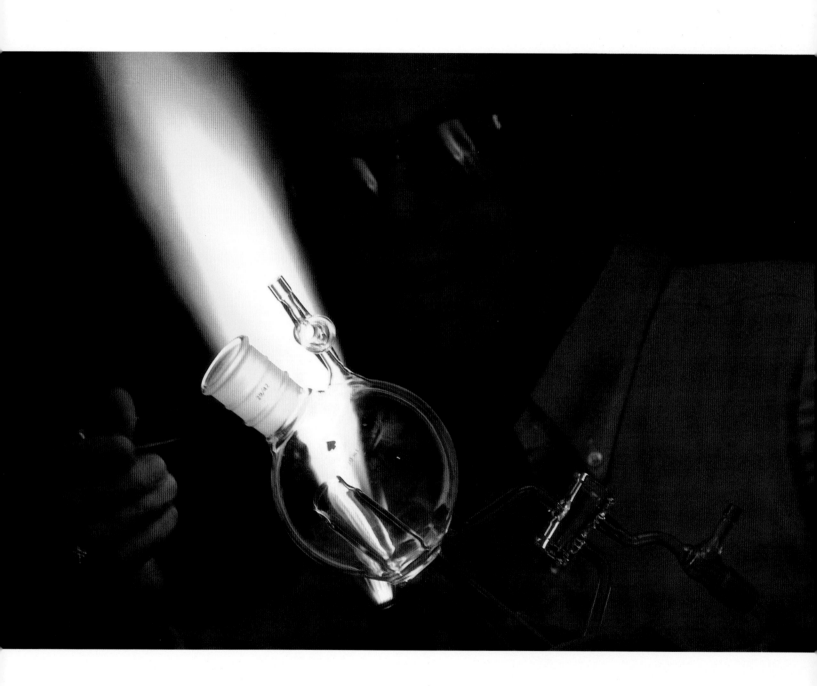

Glassblowing for chemistry research

The campus from the west, looking toward Kendall Square and Bunker Hill

Media Laboratory "computer garden"

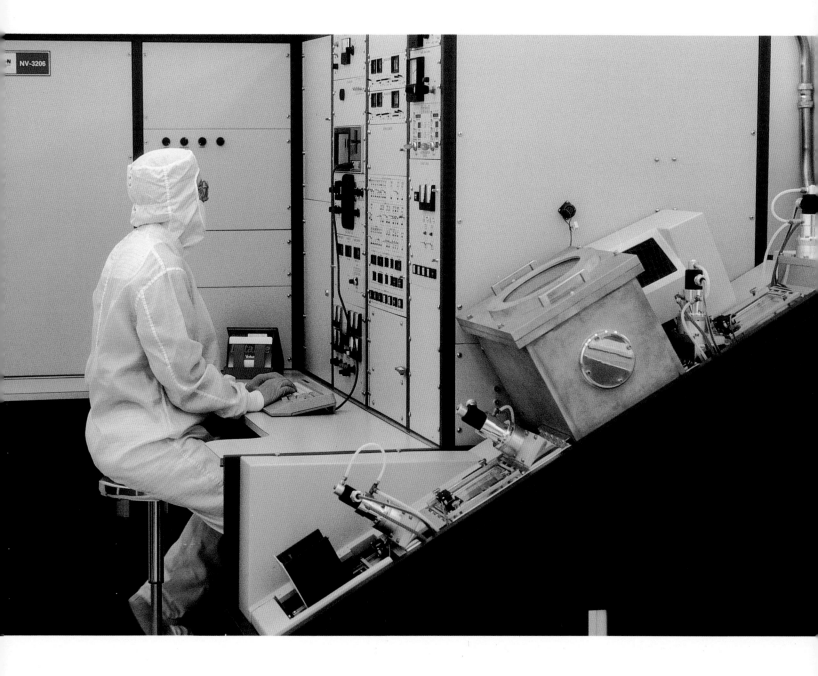

Steinbrenner Stadium and the Carr Tennis Center

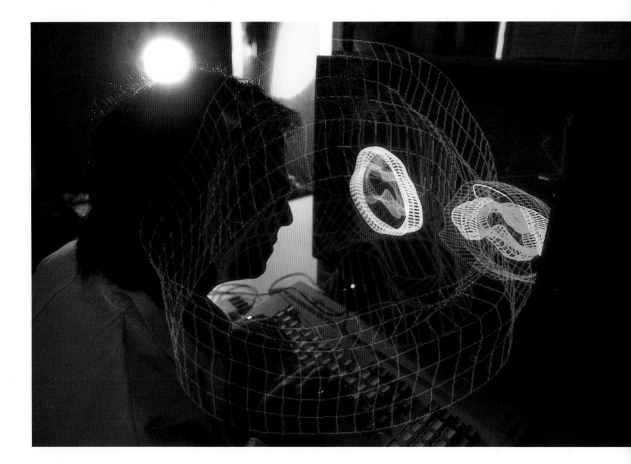

Rush Week begins on the West Campus lawn

Chi Phi, 32 Hereford Street, Boston

Rush Week cook-out, Phi Kappa Sigma

The Rogers Building (Building 7)

Freshman picnic

Freshmen arriving for orientation, Kresge Plaza

Rush Week mime

Rush party at Alpha Tau Omega

Biomechanics machine shop

Boston skyline and the Charles River Basin

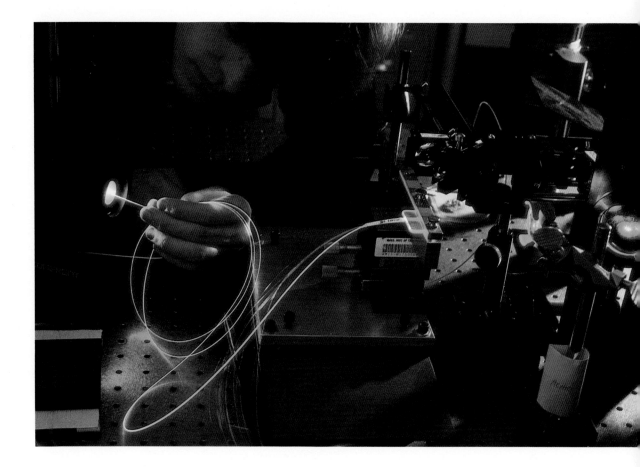

String quartet in Kresge Auditorium

Michael Heizer: "Guennette," Killian Court   *Overleaf:* Killian Court

Sunrise over the Charles River Basin

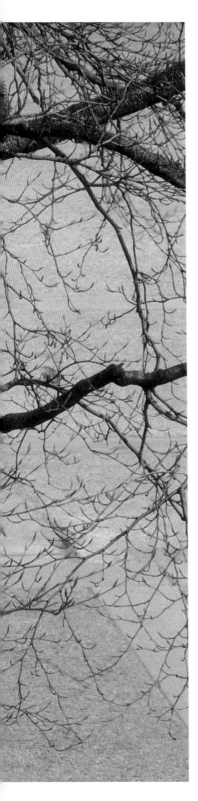

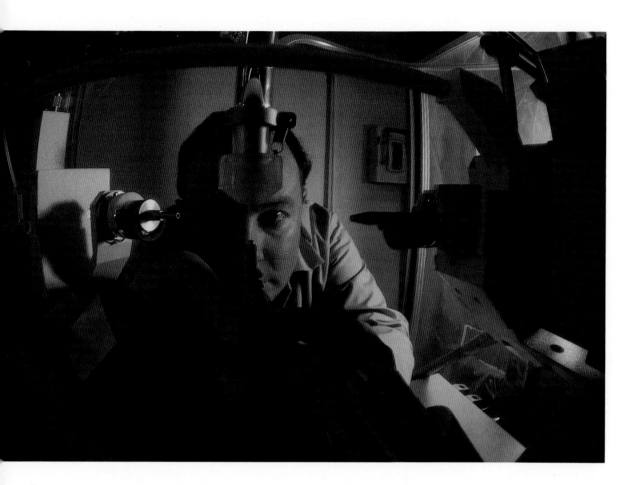

Materials Science and Engineering: single-crystal X-ray diffraction

Fall, Building 1 in Killian Court   *Overleaf:* Early morning on the Charles River

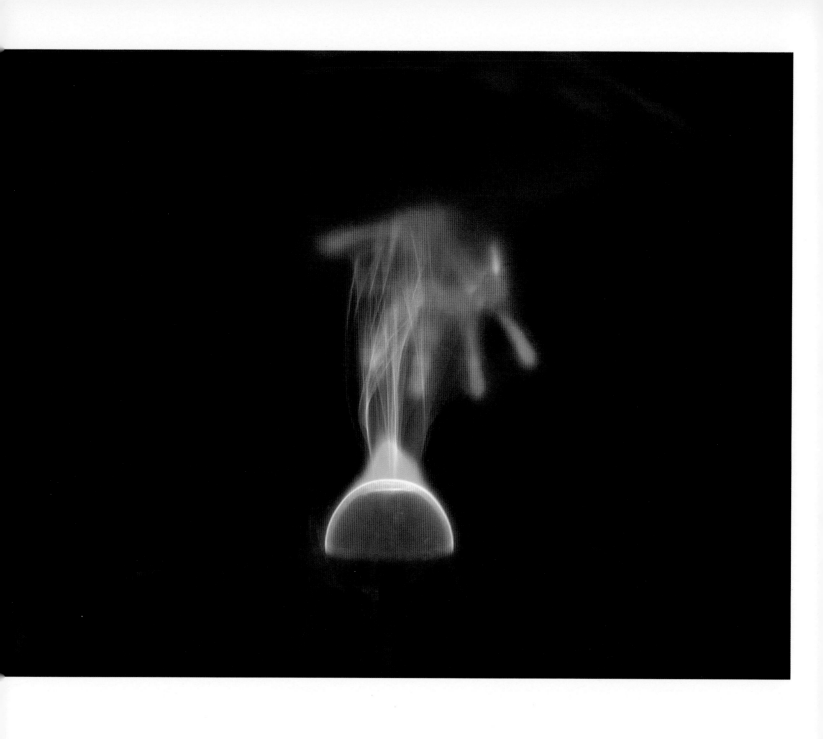

"Rights of Dawn" (1984), light sculpture by Bill Parker, '74

Wing model prepared for test, Wright Brothers Wind Tunnel

Autumn in Killian Court

The Rogers Building steps

Growing fermentation cultures for pharmaceutical research

Henry Moore: "Three-Piece Reclining Figure," Killian Court   *Overleaf:* Boston Common

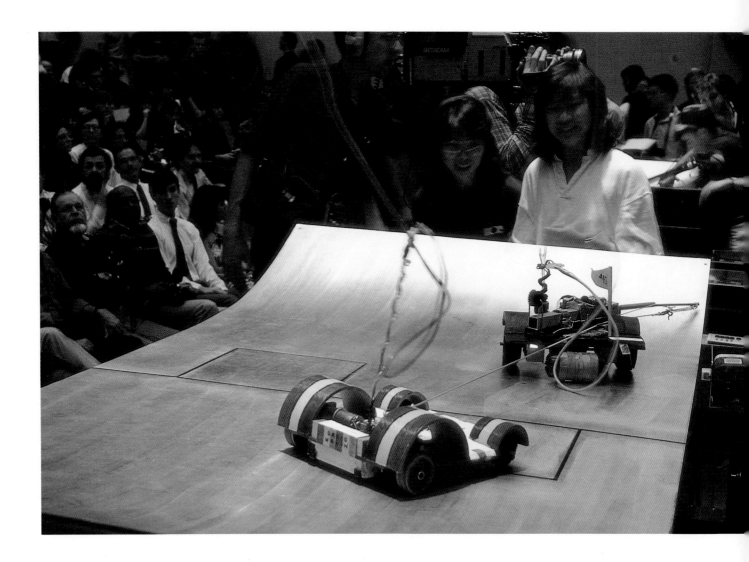

The 2.70 design contest: engineering education becomes theatre

Hayden Library

The Great Dome from Killian Court

McCormick Hall

Overleaf: The President's House Garden

The Green Building (Center for Earth Sciences) 109

Aerial view, looking south

The Green and Landau Buildings

Radio telescope on Building 26   *Overleaf:* Tech Night at the Pops, Symphony Hall

Reunions: Tech Night at the Pops

Reunion reception at the President's House   *Overleaf:* Rainy graduation in Killian Court

Graduation procession

Graduation from the Building 10 dome

President's House reunion buffet

Graduation Exercises